MINI
APARTMENT BIBLE

TECTUM
PUBLISHERS

MINI
APARTME

© 2009 Tectum Publishers
Godefriduskaai 22
2000 Antwerp
Belgium
info@tectum.be
+ 32 3 226 66 73
www.tectum.be

ISBN: 978-90-79761-08-1
WD: 2009/9021/12
(74)

Printed in China.

NT BIBLE

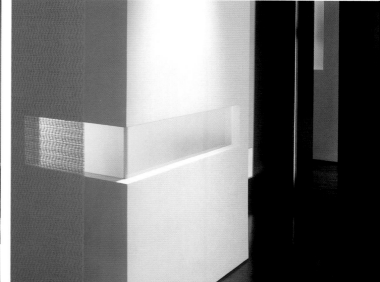

ARCHITECT Form Design Architecture • PHOTO Matthew Weinreb

ARCHITECT Tanner Leddy Maytu & Stacy Architects • PHOTO Stan Musilek & Sharon Reisdorph

ARCHITECT Michel Rojkind & Simon Hamui • PHOTO Jaime Navarro

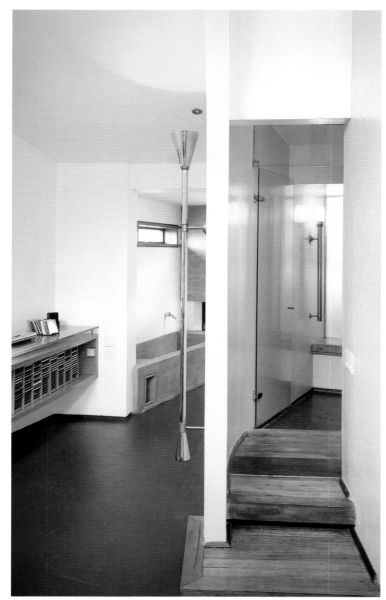

ARCHITECT Harris Hogan • PHOTO Francesca Yorke

ARCHITECT Pugh Scarpa • PHOTO Marvin Rand

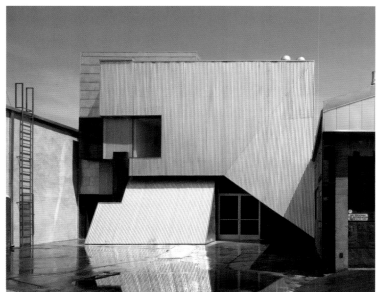

ARCHITECT Baumann Arch. PHOTO Alfonso Paredes

ARCHITECT Marcio Kogan • PHOTO Arnaldo Pappalardo

ARCHITECT Simon Conder • PHOTO Peter Warren

ARCHITECT Mark Guard • PHOTO Allan Mower

ARCHITECT Theo Hotz Architexten PHOTO Markus Fisher

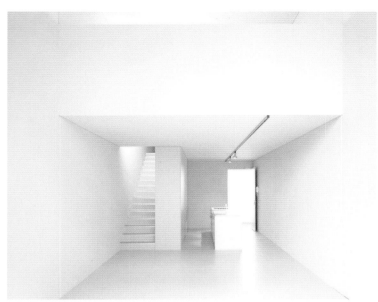

ARCHITECT **CCS Architects** • PHOTO **Javier Haddad Conde**

ARCHITECT Anthony Chan • PHOTO Virgile Simon Betrand

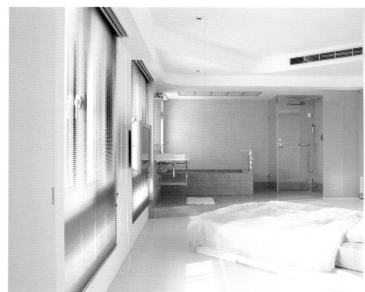

ARCHITECT **Flora de Gastines & Anne Geistdoerfer** • PHOTO **André Thoraval**

ARCHITECT MacKay & Partners • PHOTO Niall Cutton

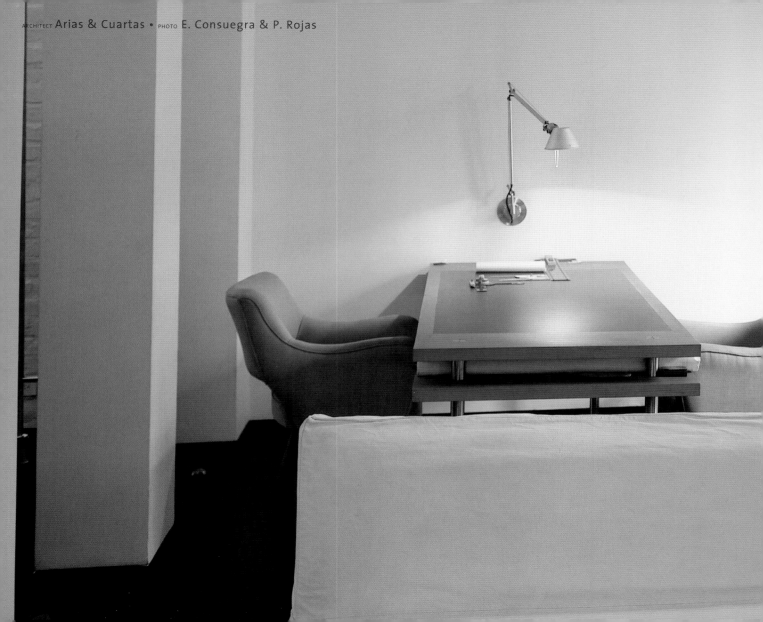

ARCHITECT Brunete Fraccaroli • PHOTO Tuca Reinés

ARCHITECT Avi Laiser & Amir Scharz • PHOTO Miri Davidovitch

ARCHITECT dRMM-de Rijke Marsh Morgan • PHOTO Michael Mack

.ARCHITECT Deadline • PHOTO Ludger Paffrath

ARCHITECT A-LDK • PHOTO Rui Morais de Sousa

ARCHITECT Daly Genik Architects • PHOTO Joshua White, Tim Street Porter

ARCHITECT **Harris Hogan Associates** • PHOTO **Francesca Yorke**

ARCHITECT Zack de Vito • PHOTO M. Bozonella

ARCHITECT Shi-Chieh Lu • PHOTO Kuomin Lee

ARCHITECT Guillermo Arias & Luis Cuartas • PHOTO E. Consuegra & P. Rojas

ARCHITECT Joshua R. Coggeshall / Cog Work Shop • PHOTO Deborah Bird, Cog Work Shop

ARCHITECT Bauart Architekten • PHOTO Andreas Greber, Hasle-Rüegsau/Weberhaus

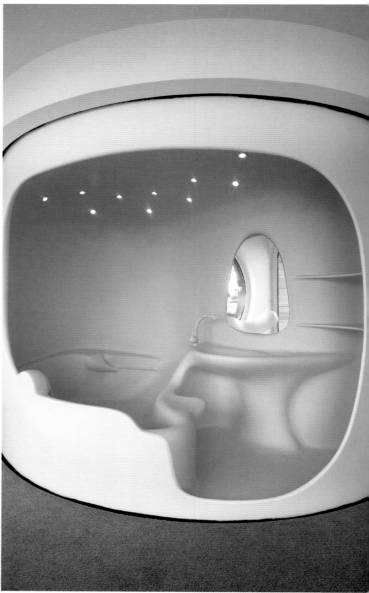

ARCHITECT Esther Hagenlocher • PHOTO Nina Siber

ARCHITECT Leonardo Annecca • PHOTO Miaz Brothers, Michael Greag

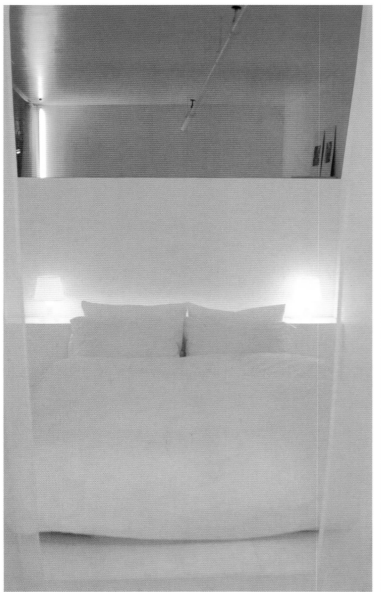

ARCHITECT Werner Aisslinger / Studio Aisslinger • PHOTO Steffen Jaenicke

ARCHITECT Cecconi Simone Inc. • PHOTO Joy von Tiedermann

ARCHITECT **Kirkpatrick Associates Architects** • PHOTO **Weldon Brewster**

ARCHITECT Guillaume Dreyfuss • PHOTO David Pisani

ARCHITECT Sopanen Sarlin • PHOTO Arno de la Chapele

ARCHITECT Franc Fernández • PHOTO Joan Mundó